GAMBEL'S QUAIL

RIO NUEVO PUBLISHERS®

P.O. Box 5250, Tucson, Arizona 85703-0250

(520) 623-9558, www.rionuevo.com

Design: Karen Schober, Seattle, Washington

Library of Congress Cataloging-in-Publication Data

Kaufman, Lynn Hassler.
  Gambel's quail / Lynn Hassler Kaufman.
    p. cm. -- (Look West)
  ISBN 1-887896-62-7 (hardcover)
  1. Gambel's quail. I. Title. II. Series.
  QL696.G259K38 2004
  598.6'27--dc22

                            2004012464

Printed in Hong Kong
10 9 8 7 6 5 4 3 2 1

GAMBEL'S QUAIL

Lynn Hassler Kaufman

LOOK WEST
SERIES

RIO NUEVO PUBLISHERS
TUCSON, ARIZONA

SITTING ON THE BACK PATIO, WATCHING
THE EVENING SHADOWS SPREAD OVER THE HILLSIDE,
WE ARE SUDDENLY STARTLED BY AN EXPLOSIVE WHIR OF
WINGS ON THE OTHER SIDE OF OUR PATIO WALL. A GROUP
OF PLUMP BIRDS ROCKETS UP FROM THE DESERT FLOOR AND,
WITH WINGS HELD STIFFLY, SAILS OVER THE HILLSIDE,
DISAPPEARING INTO THE BRUSH.

These are Gambel's quail, birds that generally walk and run on the ground, and fly only when hard pressed. Perhaps they were startled into flight by a bobcat, a snake, or any number of other threatening creatures. As the birds land on the other side of the hill, we hear much clucking and squabbling for a few minutes, and then, with the perceived danger behind them, silence falls as they conduct their final wanderings of the day. Despite the dangers inherent in the harsh environment, Gambel's quail have learned to coexist with many other desert creatures—including humans.

Few birds so capture the hearts and minds of those of us who live in the Desert Southwest. Known to even the most casual observer of nature, these conspicuous and comely creatures delight us with their captivating lifestyle. In the fall and winter Gambel's quail travel in large groups, seemingly in a state of permanent unrest as they fuss about, surveying the ground for food and water. They can be quite boisterous at times, squabbling and clucking with an almost deafening intensity. Each spring and summer, the comings and goings of the soft, fuzzy chicks scurrying around on their short legs provide hours of drama and entertainment. As the young follow their parents about, learning the ways of the world, we find that life has challenges for the newly hatched. Many of us go to great extremes to try to make life easier for the families of young, but life is hard. Each day there is one chick fewer; lost to the heat or to a predator, or simply not strong enough to survive. The attrition is heartbreaking to watch. Out of a clutch of thirteen, perhaps only three or four will survive to adulthood.

As cities in the Desert Southwest have grown, Gambel's quail have adapted to life in the suburbs, coming into our back yards to feed on scattered grain or the sweet flowers of our favorite perennials. Like coyotes and roadrunners, they have achieved near-icon status in Southwestern culture. We find depictions of them on Native American pottery, postage stamps, note and holiday cards, calendars, ceramic tiles, enameled pins, earrings and necklaces, stained glass, magnets, and fine paintings and carvings. Moreover, many a town in the Southwest has a street named after them.

THE QUAIL FAMILY

Gambel's quail are related to other chicken-like birds such as partridges, grouse, pheasants, and turkeys, but they fall within a distinct family called New World quail or Odontophoridae. Members of this family spend most of their lives on the ground and have very strong legs that make them efficient walkers and runners. Stout bills enable them to forage on the ground. They also have clawed feet with four toes, effective tools for scratching and digging for morsels to eat.

With short rounded wings, members of the Odontophoridae family are not known for their proficiency as flyers. Most prefer to remain on the

Adult male and female quail are easy to tell apart, while young chicks all look alike.

ground and are adept at hiding and crouching. They will run and hide in shrubbery rather than take to the air. If pressed to fly, they may do so, but only for short distances. Their protective coloration, coupled with their ability to take off in an instant, gives them a certain degree of protection from predators. As game birds, hunted by humans for centuries, they are instinctively wary and spook easily.

WHAT'S IN A NAME?

The scientific name for Gambel's quail is *Callipepla gambelii*. "Callipepla" comes from the Greek *kalli* meaning "beautiful" and *peplos* meaning "robe." Over the years they have been called by a variety of common names: Arizona quail, desert quail, valley quail, topknot quail, and blue quail, the latter a reference to their blue-gray backs. Hunters sometimes call them "redheads," referring to the reddish-brown caps of the males. Spanish names include *codorniz de Gambel* and *codorniz desértica*.

WHO WAS GAMBEL?

William Gambel was a naturalist from the Philadelphia Academy of Natural Sciences. While riding along the Santa Fe Trail in the early

1840s, he saw flocks of quail living in barren and brushy habitat he described as "impossible for sustaining life." After collecting specimens, he started to refer to them as "Gambel's quail." In those days it was considered improper to name a bird after oneself, but Gambel believed that his friend and mentor Thomas Nuttall had already named it thus—which in fact was not the case, but the name became official anyway.

THE DESERT IS HOME

Gambel's quail is the most arid-adapted of all the North American quail, and the heart of its range is the Sonoran Desert—central and southern Arizona and northwestern Sonora, Mexico—where it may be found year-round. These birds also inhabit desert areas of southeastern California, extreme southern Nevada, southern Utah, western Colorado, southwestern New Mexico, and extreme western Texas. Gambel's quail have been introduced to various locations, including San Clemente Island off the coast of California and the Hawaiian Islands, where a few remain today.

Because Gambel's quail attempt to run and hide when threatened, cover is important in their habitat. The birds prefer areas with

A female investigates a saguaro blossom (Saguaro National Park, Tucson, Arizona).

cactus and brushy, thorny trees and shrubs in the pea, or legume, family. They tend to be particularly abundant in regions with native mesquite trees. While these trees do not appear to be necessary for the survival of the birds, the mesquite and quail seem to thrive under the same kind of conditions. Other plants commonly found in quail territory include ironwood, saguaro, prickly pear, desert hackberry, cholla, wolfberry, brittlebush, cat's claw acacia, and burroweed. Quail also visit river valleys and drainages, as well as adjoining agricultural areas.

SNAPPY DRESSERS

Gambel's quail are elegant-looking birds with jaunty, upright top-knots. The head plume appears as one feather arising from the center of the bird's crown but is actually a set of about six black, teardrop-shaped feathers that overlap very tightly. Both the male and female have flanks sharply patterned with streaks of chestnut and white. Males have distinctive black and white patterns on the face and throat, reddish-brown crowns, and cream-colored bellies with a conspicuous black patch in the center. The female birds are less striking, lacking strong facial patterns and the black belly patch; their buff-colored (or as birders would say, "buffy") abdomens are subtly streaked with brown.

GREGARIOUS AND SOCIABLE

Throughout the fall and winter months, Gambel's quail gather in large groups called coveys. These may bring together several family

groups, with different adult pairs as well as offspring from the previous breeding season. Coveys may number twenty or more. These gregarious birds ramble about on daily circuits, searching for food and water. As some members of the covey feed or drink, others watch for signs of danger. When spring arrives, birds gradually separate from the covey and go off in pairs to breed.

SOMETHING TO TALK ABOUT

Gambel's quail have a variety of calls, each associated with a different activity or behavior.

One of the most recognizable sounds in the desert is the "call to assembly," or location call. Throughout the day, the soft, worried *ka-KAA-ka-ka* call is used by birds separated from their mates or other members of the covey. This same fretful vocalization is sometimes heard at daybreak as members of a covey reconvene after being separated at night. If flocks are widely scattered, the location call may be accompanied by a constant, anxious *whit-whit*.

When moderately alarmed, both males and females will utter a *chip-chip-chip*. This may be in response to the presence of a predator such as a bobcat, coyote, or snake, or simply concern about some suspicious or unfamiliar situation. If extremely alarmed, they emit a distressed-sounding *crear-crear* and then usually take flight.

A distinctive call associated with the reproductive process is heard beginning in the early spring. Males sit atop perches and call with a repetitive and penetrating *cre-AA-ah* as they announce their availability as mates.

WHAT'S FOR BREAKFAST?

Gambel's quail walk purposefully, wending their way through the thorny brush, picking up tidbits of food from the ground. Plant parts, particularly those from the pea family, make up most of their diet. Since some seedpods are tough and hard, quail often consume partially digested seeds found in animal droppings. In addition to seeds, they also eat leaves and grass blades throughout the year as well as the seasonal fruits of cactus such as prickly pear, saguaro, and cholla. Although primarily ground feeders, they may also fly into low shrubs or trees to feast on small fruits such as hackberry or wolfberry. They may also leap straight into the air to pluck a tasty flower from a penstemon or other plant. During the nesting season, both adult birds and their young may eat insects as well.

An adult male quail delivering his mating call.

Most feeding occurs at dawn and dusk. At first light, quail leave their nighttime roosts in trees and shrubs, re-gather as a group, and travel to a favorite feeding area or source of water. A covey may surround a stand of water, moving their heads up and down as they drink. First one bird, then another, then another drinks, lifting their

heads in order to swallow and then repeating this motion, all timed slightly differently as if orchestrated by some invisible maestro.

Greens, in the form of leaves and grass blades, make up an important part of the quail's diet. The vitamin A in greens helps trigger the

Quail sometimes eat cactus flowers, although they prefer the fruit.

hormones needed for reproduction. Following dry winters, the lack of available green plant material in the spring seems to inhibit the production of young and to lower the survival rates of young adults. Gambel's quail apparently feed heavily on filaree (*Erodium cicutarium*), an introduced weed, proving that they will adapt to new feeding opportunities.

HOT AND COLD

During blistering weather conditions, Gambel's quail may seek out shade during the hottest part of the day, perhaps under a mesquite tree or saltbush. They may also nestle into a spot of cool, damp soil and rest for an hour or two. Hollowed-out depressions in the soil provide cooling and moisture, helping to regulate hot temperatures. Birds have no sweat glands, but they cope with overheating by a mechanism called gular fluttering. With their mouths open, the birds flutter the skin on their throats. As the

air passes over the moisture in their mouths, the effect is like that of an evaporative cooler, lowering the overall temperature of the birds' bodies. During very cold conditions, the quail may fluff up their feathers to conserve body heat, or they may find a sunny spot for soaking up warmth from the sun's rays.

DUST BATHING

Quail often engage in a ritual known as dust bathing. They roll over and over in the soil, creating body-sized hollows in the dirt. They then proceed to peck and scrape the soil loose with their feet, sifting dust through their feathers. Using their wings in a shuttle-like motion, they flick dust onto their backs. This activity may help maintain their feathers. Dust bathing also helps dislodge mites, fleas, and other parasites.

SHORT-DISTANCE FLYERS

The strongest, most proficient flyers in the bird world—such as falcons, terns, and swifts—tend to have long, pointed wings. The short, rounded wings of Gambel's quail are not particularly effective for flying long distances. However, their wing structure does enable

Quail generally visit the same water sources day after day.

them to quickly burst into flight if they feel threatened. The wings of young quail develop very rapidly. While other types of birds can't fly until they're full grown, young quail can fly short distances when only a few days old and still quite small.

An enthusiastic chick perches on its mother's back.

‖ HEIGHT AT NIGHT ‖

Most North American quail spend nights on the ground. For example, the bobwhite of the East and Montezuma quail of the Southwest bed down for the night by forming a tight group circle and huddling together with individual birds facing outwards. The strategy here is that if a predator approaches, at least one member of the group should see it coming. Gambel's quail, on the other hand, seek nighttime roosting, or sleeping, sites in bushes and trees. Locations probably vary by time of year, but some favorite spots include densely branched trees and shrubs such as mesquite or hackberry. Clumps of mistletoe located high up in trees or shrubs are also used. The birds chatter incessantly, clucking and calling for ten minutes or so as they shuffle about and settle in for the night.

‖ FEISTY IN FEATHERS ‖

Quail are not inherently aggressive creatures. Most aggressive behavior takes place during the breeding season, generally in association with the presence of mates or chicks. Courting or paired males often chase other birds away during nesting season to defend their mates. Males may face off with one another, bobbing their heads and making *wit-wut* calls. If the confrontation escalates, they may fly at one another and wrestle on the ground, attempting to peck at each other's skulls. Often one bird is chased off without a fight.

Adults may chase off adolescent quail when they enter a feeding area where chicks are present. Lowering their heads, they run directly at the intruders. Neither sex defends territories, although breeding pairs do tend to spread out when foraging, in order to avoid male aggression.

‖ NEW GENERATIONS ‖

The incessant calling of the male Gambel's quail heralds the beginning of the nesting season. Normally ground-dwelling birds, males suddenly may appear on elevated perches. From trees and shrubs, fence posts, chimney tops, and even evaporative coolers, they perch on high and utter a distinctive *cre-AA-ah* call that may go on all day long. This attention-seeking behavior advertises the bachelor male's availability to the opposite sex.

Calling by males may begin as early as February and may last into summer, but the peak calling period seems to be mid-April to early May. In years of extreme drought, when conditions are not particularly favorable due to food shortages, calling may be delayed or nonexistent. During wet years when more food in the form of plant material is available, calling may begin earlier and may be more concentrated.

QUAIL TO QUAIL

Gambel's quail form traditional pairs, with male and female remaining together for most of their adult lives. Males engage in a courtship display, which often begins with a lot of nudging and prodding when the birds are still within their wintertime coveys. Later on in the spring, courtship becomes more intense.

When male and female meet, the male utters a series of *wit-wut* calls accompanied by much head bobbing. As the female approaches, the male stands with his legs fully extended, exposing his eye-catching black belly patch. He may fluff out his feathers, fan his tail, and slope his body downward from tail to head with his beak close to the ground. As he bows and bobs his head, the plumes of his topknot vibrate, exposing his rusty head patch. Sometimes a male will also engage in a courtship ritual called "tidbitting," in which he offers the female choice bits of food in an attempt to win her over.

CHOOSING A NEST SITE

Females generally select the nest site, most often on the ground, concealed under a shrub or some other form of cover. The female scratches out a shallow basin, often bordering it with small twigs. The bowl-shaped scrape may be sparsely lined with grass, leaves, or feathers. Nests are occasionally found in unusual places such as on top of a wood rat den or within the center of a dead agave. Sometimes they are placed off the ground in a tree or shrub. In more urban settings, potted plants provide a popular venue.

EGGS APLENTY

Females usually lay ten to twelve eggs, white to buffy in color, with splotches of brown. As many as twenty eggs have been recorded. In dry years there tend to be fewer. If you find a nest with more than fifteen eggs, more than one female may be responsible. This is a phenomenon called "dump nesting." Females may lay their eggs in another female's nest because they don't have one of their own, or because the urgency of laying an egg is such that it must be laid immediately.

Normal egg-laying occurs at intervals of twenty-five to twenty-eight hours. After laying four to six eggs, the female often takes a day off without laying an egg, and then the cycle begins anew. The clutch is most often complete after about three of these cycles.

Hatching day.

The female is usually the only incubator and begins sitting on the nest after all eggs have been laid. She incubates for about twenty-one to twenty-three days. Meanwhile, the male acts as a sentinel, keeping surveillance and patrolling nearby for the slightest sign of danger.

If something disastrous happens to the female, the male may take over the task of incubating. This happened one year in a potted coral fountain plant in my front courtyard. The female seemed to have been taken by a bobcat, for only a scattering of feathers remained. The male proved to be an able incubator, sitting on the eggs for an additional week, and the hatch was successful. Four downy young survived the trauma. I still marvel at this incredible instinct to bring off young and perpetuate the species.

HATCHING

Just prior to hatching, quail chicks begin "peeping" to one another through the eggshells. Each chick cuts a circle around the inside of its eggshell, leaving a small piece of membrane attached to the shell,

This many eggs may have come from more than one female.

which acts as a hinge as the emerging chick pushes outward. Hatching generally takes one to two hours. The young chicks emerge with their eyes open and bodies covered with down. After drying off, they are ready to leave the nest within a few short hours, led on into the big wide world by their trusty parents.

Newly hatched quail chicks begin walking almost immediately.

The downy covering lasts about two weeks and insulates their bodies as well as providing camouflage. Newly hatched quail are only partially dependent on their parents for food and care. They are what is called precocial. The word comes from the Latin *praecox* (meaning "early ripening"). Precocial chicks usually hatch in nests on or close to the ground, and their ability to run and hide (or swim—ducks are also precocial) and to feed themselves is part of their protection.

Sometimes a few unhatched eggs will remain in the nest. These may be infertile, underdeveloped, or possibly recognized as coming from another female and consequently pushed aside. However, nature leaves nothing to waste; the cracked eggshells and unhatched eggs may be cleaned up by ants or other scavengers.

‖ THERE'S A QUAIL IN MY POT! ‖

Mated pairs of quail spend a great deal of time exploring territory, prospecting for good nesting sites. As many a Southwestern homeowner can attest, Gambel's quail have a particular affinity for nesting in large flowerpots—often inconveniently located in high-traffic areas. This may cause considerable alteration of one's lifestyle

Foraging for insects.

in the interest of causing as little disturbance as possible for the nesting birds.

One year a female placed her nest in a potted geranium immediately adjacent to my front door. Avoiding the main entrance to my home proved a challenge. Besides the traffic disruption, a second downside was that my geranium plant needed water to survive—and frequently at that, during the hot summer months. Discerning how and when to water presented its challenges. I watched the comings and goings of my geranium-pot female and determined that she was off the nest first thing in the morning, at which point I would dash outside and carefully water around the eggs. One friend of mine in a similar situation ingeniously used a funnel to direct the water to an area of the plant away from the eggs.

Another concern was how, after hatching, the young fuzzballs would maneuver their way down the side of the pot. Imagine beginning your life on earth by careening down a two-foot-high flowerpot.

Hatching day for my geranium pot clutch arrived. I began to hear little cheeping noises. As I stood riveted at my window, I noticed the adult female was out of the flowerpot, pacing and crying persistently, alternating with soft clucking sounds, apparently vocalizing to coax the chicks out of the eggs. The male paced about from his sentinel position on the roof of the house. The female leaped in and out of the flowerpot numerous times over a period of one to two hours. Finally, she remained in the pot. Apparently the chicks were hatching one by one and the female was splaying her wings to warm them in preparation for their first big event in life—safely reaching the ground.

I was forced to turn away briefly to answer the insistent ring of the telephone. Upon my return to the unfolding drama, I found eleven chicks scrambling about in my front courtyard. Somehow I had missed the mighty tumble from the pot—their first big adventure in life.

It has become an annual inner conflict for me. As much as I love to watch the entire courtship, nesting, and hatching process, I fuss about the welfare of the parents and the chicks. Being a plant lover, I also worry about the lives of my plants. I must admit, reluctantly, that in the early months of spring, when the calls of the males may be heard from their elevated perches, I start watching my flowerpots with great vigilance. When a handsome pair of quail comes by to investigate the suitability of my pots for nesting, I gently, and with some remorse, chase them away. Of course, there are all those hours of the day when I am not home to spot an investigating pair, so surely they could still nest there. Deep inside there is a secret hope that in my absence they will choose a potted plant in my patio, so that I can once again experience the great wonder of a new generation facing the odds.

║ LIFE AS A CHICK ║

The newly hatched chicks, covered with down, begin to follow their parents around, imitating everything they do. They scratch the ground, peck for seeds, bathe in the dust, nibble on their feathers, and generally imitate everything their parents do. Adults entice the chicks to food by pecking at tidbits on the ground, and the little wind-up fuzzballs generally rush to the site. For the first few days of their lives, the young feed on grit and tiny insects, which provide a source of protein. Eventually they are able to digest seeds, which they prefer.

Females are typically more involved with feeding, while males spend more time as sentinels, guarding the group and watching for predators and other dangerous situations. Newly hatched young may

become easily chilled during their first few days and will often burrow into the fluffed-out body feathers of either parent in order to stay warm. With their fast-moving legs, they seem to disappear mysteriously and are able to hide in places that seem impossible. On command from their parents, they will freeze in their tracks and remain motionless or else run for cover.

GOOD PARENTS/BAD PARENTS

As with other species (including our own), good parenting is not a skill possessed by all Gambel's quail. Chicks may become separated from their parents or other members of the brood. Adult quail sometimes abandon their young, or one or two may be unable to keep up and are left behind as the parents and stronger chicks scurry away into new territory. It's a common but painful sight to see one or two babies running along, cheeping frantically, with no parents in sight.

Fortunately, some adults seem to have better instincts for parenting. These dutiful parents are fearless in their defense of the downy young, rarely leaving their sides and herding them closely. They will charge forward to scare away other birds or lizards. Both adults will splay their wings and sit on the young to keep them safe and warm.

If the young become permanently separated from their parents, they may be gathered up by other broods or joined by unpaired individuals. Pairs and single adults may care for very large broods composed of chicks of mixed ages.

Abandoned chicks are not necessarily doomed. One year three small, apparently parentless chicks in my neighborhood survived on their own. Despite predatory dangers, this threesome—two males and one female—managed to beat the odds. Every day when the "three musketeers" came to drink at my birdbath, they were larger and stronger. They grew up and finally disappeared into the adult community.

Young quail are not fully independent until about $2\frac{1}{2}$–3 months after hatching, and they seldom move far from where they were hatched. For the first year, the young generally stay with their parents and forage and roost as a family covey through the winter. Young birds usually form pair bonds late in their first winter and breed in early spring.

Hatching success varies by year. Adults may not breed at all in some years. Egg and chick mortality appears to be higher in dry years than wet ones. Reproductive failure may be caused by

Quail pairs tend to mate for life.

absence of rain-induced plant growth, since green food is so important to the reproductive process. However, even after successive

years of reasonably wet winters, there may still be poor hatching success. The quail may be unable to sustain high levels of reproductive performance year after year. They seem to be adapted to the boom/bust existence so typical of regions in the Southwest, with their changing cycles of wet and dry. In good years, the laying of so many eggs is an adaptation for species survival. Despite the odds, generally a few chicks will survive.

ENEMIES AND LIFE EXPECTANCY

The mean life expectancy of Gambel's quail is only $1\frac{1}{2}$ years, and they rarely live more than four years. Bobcats, Cooper's hawks, and Harris's hawks are all reported to be predators of both adults and young. However, more substantial losses appear to be due to egg robbers—small mammals such as round-tailed ground squirrels and snakes. Gila monsters also occasionally eat quail eggs, and roadrunners may eat the tiny chicks as well as the eggs.

Generally, quail avoid their predators by running, flushing, or hiding. When incubating on the nest, they often freeze and hold tight, but if pressed too close will flush and abandon nest and eggs.

Teenage quail still look pretty scruffy.

‖ BRINGING UP THE REAR ‖

Of the many Native American legends about coyotes and quail, none describe the intriguing behavior of quail tailing a single coyote. Although coyotes are not known to be important predators of quail, they must pose some sort of threat. Over the years, I've watched coveys of quail closely following a coyote, within a foot or two of its tail. While tailing they squabble, cluck, and carry on in an obviously agitated manner. The coyote just trots along, never turning to attack, but occasionally looking back over his shoulder. It is as if the quail are taunting the bully.

I still puzzle over this behavior, but I am continually amazed at life and death in the desert. A covey may be twenty feet away from a bobcat that suddenly appears from the cover of a mesquite, but the two do not meet. The quail's camouflage, wariness, and ability to take flight on a dime combine to save them.

Contemporary ceramic plate by potter Miriam Gallegos of Mata Ortiz, Mexico.

OF QUAIL AND HUMANS

Native American peoples historically trapped quail for food and for their feathers, to use for decoration. Anglo Americans also trapped quail for commercial and personal use until the end of the nineteenth century, when trapping became illegal. The hunting of quail with shotguns continues to be a popular pursuit to the present day. Fortunately, populations of Gambel's quail in the United States have remained fairly stable since the 1960s.

Many Native American tribes have traditionally used images of birds, including quail, on pottery. Classic Black-on-white Mimbres pottery—much of it produced from A.D. 1000 to 1150—reflects stylized imagery of quail. Scenes on the pottery of other tribes show masked figures hunting turkey and quail, as well as mammals.

Native American artists continue to take their inspiration from nature. Today you can find Hopi kachina carvings of quail, as well as Zuni fetishes and other

Quail motifs painted on Middle Gila buff ware sherds from the Snaketown site near Phoenix, Arizona (A.D. 900–1450, Hohokam culture).

tribes' folk art. These elegant birds are pictured on handmade, traditional pots of Mata Ortiz in northern Mexico, as well as on Acoma pottery. Zuni necklaces have also used quail motifs.

Modern hunters continue to hunt Gambel's quail, but numbers are controlled by strict bag limits. State game and fish departments monitor populations to make sure they can sustain the yearly harvests. Nowadays, it appears that the number of people who eat quail is fewer than the number of people who feed them.

‖ ATTRACTING QUAIL TO THE HOME GARDEN ‖

Quality of habitat appears to be a primary factor for attracting these birds. An important component is overhead shrubbery that screens the birds from the sun and shields them from predators. When forced to flee dangerous situations, Gambel's quail like to retreat to dense cover where they feel safe. Trees such as mesquite and acacia

Hohokam Santa Cruz Red-on-buff plate from the Snaketown site (A.D. 900–1200).

An 1846 painting by C. C. A. Christensen depicts Mormons camping near Nauvoo, Illinois, on their way to Utah. According to the account, a miracle occurred as flocks of quail landed at the camp, providing the hungry pioneers with food.

both fit the bill. Shrubs such as saltbush are also excellent. Moreover, trees and shrubs provide shade and sites for nighttime roosting.

Probably less important is the provision of food. If you live in an area of natural desert, there is probably plenty of natural food for the quail to eat. But bird feeding remains a popular pastime for many of us. Remember that by scattering seeds and grain, rather than placing it all in one area, you will provide a more natural way for the birds to forage. Quail blocks, despite the name, attract more than just quail. Javelinas, pack rats, and other less desirable animals also find these blocks of seed delicious. Sometimes the javelinas will roll the blocks over and over with their snouts, so that they end up far from their original location.

Quail seem to have a sweet tooth and like to feed on buds and flowers, particularly daleas, penstemons, and salvias, so planting some of these flowering perennials may help to attract them. An area of loose dirt under a shrub or tree will encourage dust bathing and midday resting places.

A simple birdbath or water feature will be a welcomed addition. I use an inexpensive planter dish that I clean out every day with a wire brush. If you keep the water on the shallow side, smaller birds will visit it too.

Males often perch on fence posts so females will notice them.

‖ OTHER NORTH AMERICAN QUAIL ‖

CALIFORNIA QUAIL

Callipepla californica • Spanish: *codorniz californiana*

California quail, the state bird of its namesake, is the Gambel's closest relative. Most common in open oak woodland, California quail also live in suburbs, areas of semi-desert, piñon-juniper woodland, grassland, and coastal sage, primarily in Washington, Oregon, California, and Baja California, Mexico. We find localized populations in British Columbia, Idaho, Utah, and Nevada as well. The ranges of these two closely related birds do overlap in parts of California, Utah, and northwestern Mexico.

Male California quail are boldly patterned with black and white faces with buff-yellow on the head. The rear of the crown and nape are brown, unlike the Gambel's cinnamon color. Six forward-facing, comma-shaped black plumes form a curved topknot. California quail also have black scaling on the underparts, brownish-gray flanks (unlike the chestnut of Gambel's), and black streaking on the neck.

These stately birds move seasonally within their home range, searching for food. They scratch on the ground for seeds and may

California quail.

also jump straight off the ground to garner a tasty flower or bud. Their strong bills can shell acorns and sunflower seeds. They generally roost off the ground in groups but will sometimes spend the night on the ground.

MOUNTAIN QUAIL

Oreortyx pictus • Spanish: *codorniz de montaña*

John Muir called mountain quail the "lonely mountaineer" about which little was known. This remains true today. These mysterious and elusive birds live in dense shrub and forest habitats, and breed at high elevations in the Sierra, Cascade, and Coast ranges of the West. Unlike other North American quail, they often migrate, although only for short distances. Migrating by foot, they move to lower elevations for winter to avoid snow.

Mountain quail are smartly patterned, with long, straight, black head plumes and gray crowns and crests, with chestnut throat patches bordered in black and white. Broad white bars adorn their chestnut sides. If approached they remain motionless in the brush, where they are very difficult to see. They are most conspicuous in

Mountain quail.

spring, when the rich call notes of the males may be heard echoing across the slopes. Mountain quail are fond of seeds, bulbs, leaves, berries, acorns, insects, and greens. They often scratch among the leaf litter for food and use their feet to dig for tasty bulbs.

SCALED QUAIL

Callipepla squamata • Spanish: *codorniz escamosa, codorniz azul*

Scaled quail reside in the grassy plains in southeastern and south-central Arizona, New Mexico, west Texas, and the central plateau of Mexico. Some birds range as far north as southeastern Colorado and southwestern Kansas, as well as in the Texas and Oklahoma panhandles.

The name "scaled" refers to the distinctive scalloping on the uniformly bluish-gray bodies of these birds. They are also fondly known as "cottontops," a reference to the short, bushy white crests on the birds' heads. Scaled quail females are slightly browner and duller than the males, but the two sexes are essentially identical in appearance.

Scaled quail.

Cottontop coveys often exist miles from permanent water, which does not seem to be essential to their day-to-day survival. However, they do drink freely when water is available. Principal foods include seeds, grass blades, grains, grasshoppers, and other insects.

The downy young of scaled quail may be seen as late as mid-September and even into October. They don't normally raise two broods per season; they simply delay nesting until conditions are suitable. The destruction of grasslands due to drought, fire suppression, and overgrazing remains a threat to this species.

MONTEZUMA QUAIL, HARLEQUIN QUAIL

Cyrtonyx montezumae • Spanish: *codorniz Moctezuma*

This is essentially a Mexican species, but some populations of Montezuma quail extend across the border to the mountain grasslands of southwestern Texas, southwestern New Mexico, and southeastern Arizona.

Males are stunning creatures with white and black puffy heads with a clownish appearance, dark expressive eyes, and russet-colored bushy crests. Pale blue beaks complete their otherworldly appearance.

Montezuma quail.

Brown and black checks interlaced with white adorn their backs, while their underparts are a rich mahogany that turns to black at the rump. Females are cinnamon colored with brown, black, and buff markings. Both sexes have strong feet and scythe-shaped claws specialized for digging out the bulbs of nut grasses. Despite their bold pattern, they blend in well with their surroundings and are particularly wary and difficult to observe.

Although Montezuma quail begin pairing off as early as February or March, nesting doesn't actually begin until late June, July, or August, when the summer rainy season arrives. Nesting activity appears to be related to the increased humidity of that season, as well as the emergence of new plant growth and increase in the number of insects, an important dietary item at this time.

These shy, secretive birds are reluctant to leave their grassy wooded areas. They will lie low in the grass until almost stepped upon, then burst into the air with a startling roar of wings. Like other grassland-dwelling birds, Montezuma quail roost on the ground at night. These birds were previously more widespread, but livestock grazing and summer droughts have taken their toll.

NORTHERN BOBWHITE

Colinus virginianus • Spanish: *codorniz cotuf*

Northern bobwhite is the only quail native to eastern North America. It also resides in parts of Mexico and the Caribbean. Populations of these birds in southeastern and midwestern states have been on the decline for the past thirty years, primarily due to habitat loss. Bobwhites seem to prefer the early successional plant life following disturbances from fire, timber harvesting, and agriculture. Today the densest populations are in southern pine forests that are managed specifically for bobwhite hunting and in the rangelands of southern Texas, during periods of above-average rainfall.

Northern bobwhite.

In typical bobwhite populations in North America, the male has a white throat and eyebrow, setting off the black face and chest, but there is much variation among bobwhites in Mexico. Bobwhites feed on seed but are opportunistic and also dine on many insects as well as spiders and centipedes in the summer season. The whistled *bob-WHITE!* vocalization is a familiar sound in the spring. Ground nesters, these birds often set up housekeeping close to openings in the woods such as roads or fields.

MASKED BOBWHITE

Colinus virginianus ridgwayi • Spanish: *codorniz mascarata*

A subspecies of northern bobwhite, masked bobwhite is noteworthy because it was discovered late—in the 1880s—but disappeared from its limited Arizona range by the early 1900s, before ornithologists really had time to study its life history. Its range was limited to plains and river valleys in Sonora, Mexico, and grassy areas in extreme south-central Arizona, an area that underwent a period of drought in 1885–86. Drought conditions, coupled with overgrazing of livestock, stripped the area bare of vegetation, and

Masked bobwhite.

masked bobwhites began to disappear. In 1985 the U.S. Fish and Wildlife Service purchased the Buenos Aires Ranch in the Altar Valley of south-central Arizona and began a reintroduction effort using bobwhites from the remnant population in Sonora, Mexico.

As with other Southwestern quail, the summer rainy season is important for the nesting activities of masked bobwhite. The increased production of green growth provides both food and cover, and increased numbers of insects help support adults and their offspring.

Male birds are a rich chestnut brown with black heads and throats, and are smaller than more northerly races of bobwhite. Females and young birds lack the solid black or chestnut, and have whitish to pale buff-colored throats and buffy bodies barred with black.

‖ SUGGESTED READING ‖

Brown, David E. *Arizona Game Birds.* Tucson, Arizona: University of
    Arizona Press and Arizona Game and Fish Department, 1989.
Kaufman, Kenn. *Lives of North American Birds.* Boston, Massachusetts:
    Houghton Mifflin Co., 1996.
Kaufman, Lynn Hassler. *Birds of the American Southwest.* Tucson, Arizona:
    Rio Nuevo Publishers, 2000.
Russell, Stephen M., and Gale Monson. *The Birds of Sonora.*
    Tucson, Arizona: University of Arizona Press, Tucson, 1998.

‖ PHOTOGRAPHY © AS FOLLOWS: ‖

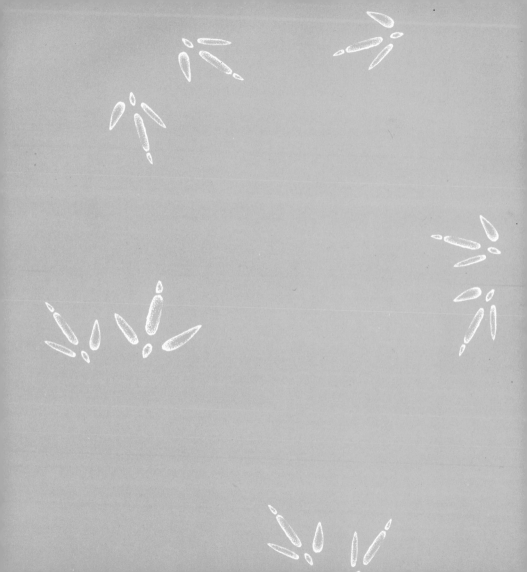